THE SCIENCE OF
SWIMMING

By
Emilie Dufresne

PLAY
SMART

BookLife
PUBLISHING

©2019
BookLife Publishing
King's Lynn
Norfolk PE30 4LS
All rights reserved.
Printed in Malaysia.

A catalogue record for this
book is available from the
British Library.

ISBN: 978-1-78637-531-5

Written by:
Emilie Dufresne

Edited by:
Kirsty Holmes

Designed by:
Gareth Liddington

Photocredits:

Cover – Boris Ryaposov, JaySi, E. O., ConstantinosZ, Peruskyi Petro, wavebreakmedia. 2 - Snapper 68. 4 - seyomedo. 5 - Focon. 6 - studioloco.
7 - Pavel L Photo and Video. 8 - Erica Smit. 9 - Elena.Degano. 10 - EpicStockMedia. 11 - frantisehojdysz. 12 - Jacob Lund. 13 - Solis Images.
14 - Microgen. 15 - Stone36. 16 - Be Good. 17 - altanaka. 18 - Olesia Bilkei. 19 - captainmilos. 20 - Dreams Come True. 21 - Wallenrock.
22 - Andrienko Anastasiya, ThomasLENNE. 23 - Be Good, Olesia Bilkei, altanaka.

Images are courtesy of Shutterstock.com. With thanks to Getty Images, Thinkstock Photo and iStockphoto.

All facts, statistics, web addresses and URLs in this book were verified as valid and accurate at time of writing.
No responsibility for any changes to external websites or references can be accepted by either the author or publisher.

CONTENTS

Words that look like **this** can be found in the glossary on page 24.

LET'S GO SWIMMING!

Are you ready to learn all about the **forces**, patterns and angles behind swimming? Then grab your goggles and towel, the water is lovely!

Swimming is a sport where you pull and push yourself through the water using your hands and legs.

Some swimming sports include racing, diving and **synchronised** (say: sink-RON-ize-d) swimming.

AIR VS WATER

You have to move differently in water than on land because water has a higher density than air. When on land, the biggest force acting on us is gravity, which pulls us towards the centre of the Earth.

Density means how closely-packed the **molecules** in a material are.

GRAVITY

Buoyancy (say: boy-an-see) is the force that pushes objects in liquids upwards.

BUOYANT FORCE

Water has a higher density than air. This means that it is harder to move through it. However, in certain positions, we can float on water. This is because of buoyancy.

FABULOUS FLOATING

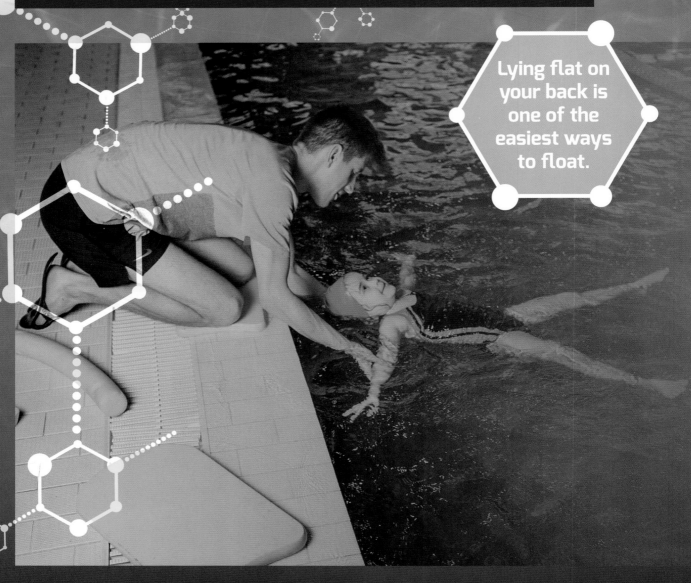

Lying flat on your back is one of the easiest ways to float.

Any object that is less dense than water will float on it. Humans are only slightly less dense than water. This means that we can sink or float. Getting into certain positions can help you float.

When you lie on your back it makes your **surface area** larger. The more surface area you create, the more area there is that the buoyant force can push upwards on. The less surface area you take up, the more you will sink.

Stretch your arms out at right angles from your body to help you balance.

SCARED OF SINKING?

Sinking isn't scary when you know how to do it. When you are standing in the water, pull your legs up to your chest. This will make your surface area smaller and you will start to sink.

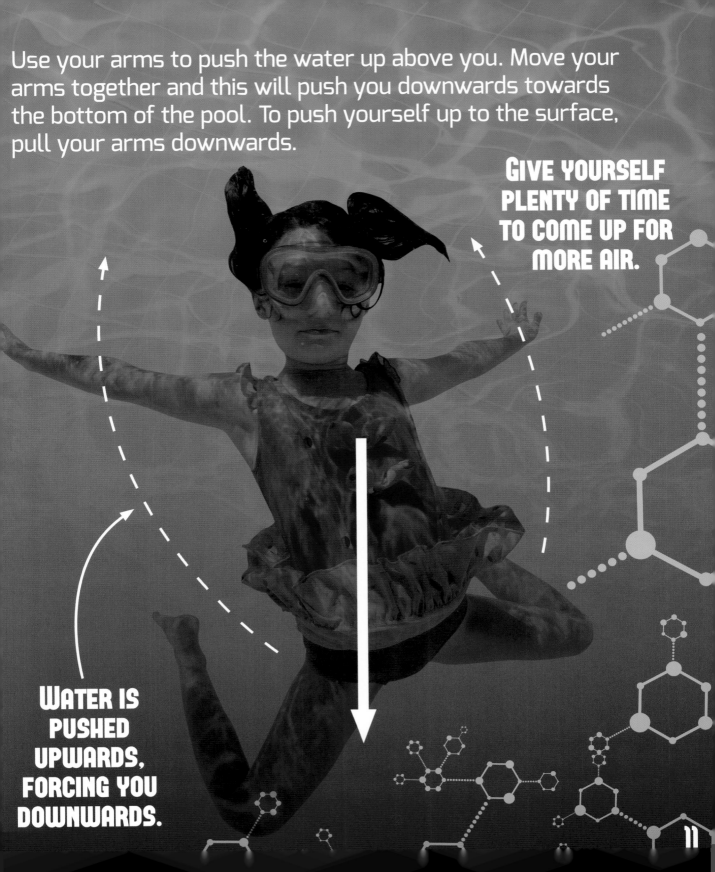

Use your arms to push the water up above you. Move your arms together and this will push you downwards towards the bottom of the pool. To push yourself up to the surface, pull your arms downwards.

GIVE YOURSELF PLENTY OF TIME TO COME UP FOR MORE AIR.

WATER IS PUSHED UPWARDS, FORCING YOU DOWNWARDS.

THE PERFECT PUSH-OFF

The perfect push-off will give you a speedy start to your swim. Push-offs are all about energy and friction.

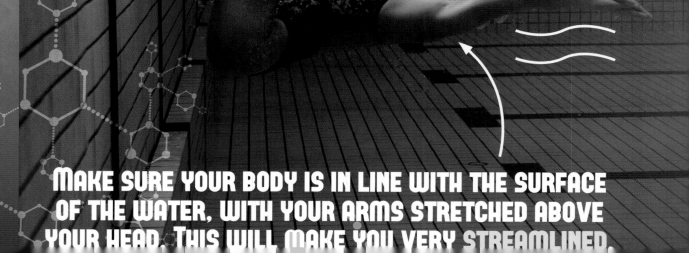

BEND YOUR LEGS SLIGHTLY SMALLER THAN A RIGHT ANGLE. THIS GETS YOUR MUSCLES READY TO PUT LOTS OF ENERGY INTO YOUR PUSH.

MAKE SURE YOUR BODY IS IN LINE WITH THE SURFACE OF THE WATER, WITH YOUR ARMS STRETCHED ABOVE YOUR HEAD. THIS WILL MAKE YOU VERY STREAMLINED.

When you push off from the wall, there is friction between your feet and the wall.

AS YOU PUSH YOUR FEET AGAINST THE WALL, THE WALL PUSHES BACK AGAINST YOUR FEET.

THE MUSCLES IN YOUR LEGS CREATE LOTS OF ENERGY. THIS FORCES YOU FORWARD.

Friction is what happens when two things rub against and **resist** each other.

JUST KEEP SWIMMING

Swimming strokes are all about patterns and forces. Let's take a closer look at front crawl.

WHEN YOUR HAND IS UNDER THE WATER, MAKE AN 'S' SHAPE ALONG YOUR BODY.

THIS WILL GIVE YOU LOTS OF LIFT AND SPEED.

When swimming front crawl, make sure your body is straight in the water and your legs aren't hanging down at an angle. This will create more drag.

DRAG IS WHEN THE WATER HITS YOUR LEGS AND CREATES MORE RESISTANCE, PULLING YOU BACKWARDS WHEN YOU TRY TO PUSH FORWARDS.

JUMPING IN!

When you jump into the pool, your body takes up the space where the water is. All the water that used to be where your body is now splashes upwards and outwards. This is called displacement.

THE SMALLER YOU CAN MAKE THE SPOT WHERE YOU ENTER THE WATER, CALLED THE ENTRY POINT, THE SMALLER THE SPLASH WILL BE.

Always have an adult with you when jumping into the pool.

SMALL ENTRY POINT ⟶

Jumping into the water in a star shape makes your entry point much larger. Your body will take up more space in the water and more water will be displaced.

A bigger entry point means a bigger splash!

LARGE ENTRY POINT

CANNONBALL!

A cannonball is a type of jump that can create one of the biggest splashes. Making the biggest splash is all about your forces and shapes.

HEIGHT

The higher you jump, the more speed and **momentum** you will build up as you fall towards the water. This means you will hit the water with more force.

MOMENTUM

Bring your knees up and get into a ball shape. This shape displaces the most amount of water in the shortest amount of time.

A BALL SHAPE HAS A LARGE SURFACE AREA THAT DISPLACES LOTS OF WATER.

A DOWNWARDS FORCE PULLS YOU QUICKLY INTO THE WATER.

The best shape and the highest speed will make the biggest splash!

DARING DIVING

Diving properly can be tricky. The science behind the perfect dive is all about forces and angles.

OVERLAP YOUR HANDS ABOVE YOUR HEAD AND STRETCH OUT YOUR ARMS INTO A TRIANGLE SHAPE.

THIS MAKES YOU A VERY STREAMLINED SHAPE THAT WILL EASILY SLIDE INTO THE WATER.

BEND YOUR LEGS SO THAT YOUR MUSCLES ARE READY TO PUSH YOU INTO THE AIR.

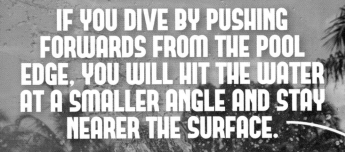

IF YOU DIVE BY PUSHING FORWARDS FROM THE POOL EDGE, YOU WILL HIT THE WATER AT A SMALLER ANGLE AND STAY NEARER THE SURFACE.

If you do a high dive and hit the water straight, you will travel straight down.

When you dive, you travel through the water at the same

SEE THE SCIENCE

Let's try an experiment! To see the science of swimming in action, you will need:

GOGGLES

A POOL

A SWIMMING COSTUME

Try jumping in the pool whilst making different shapes. Which shapes made the biggest splash? Which ones made you fall deep into the water? Here are some shapes to get you started:

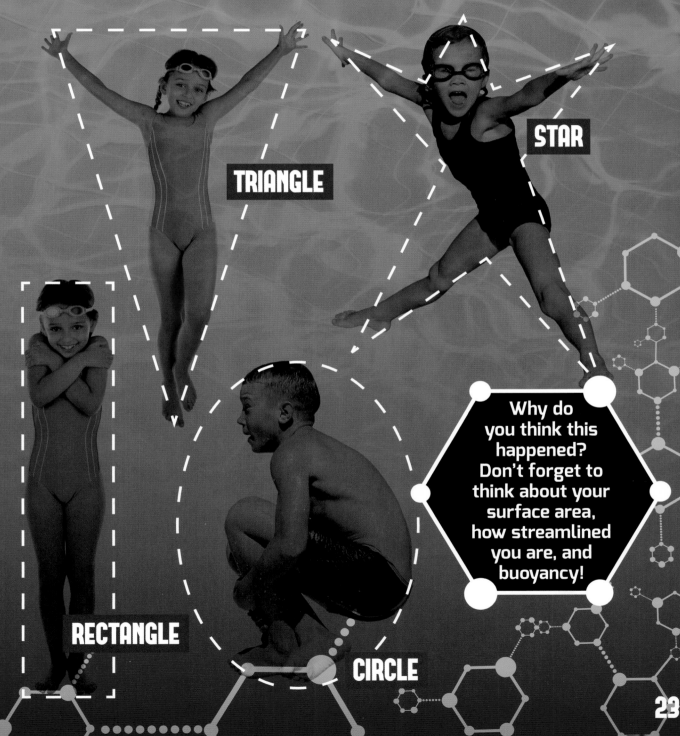

TRIANGLE

STAR

RECTANGLE

CIRCLE

Why do you think this happened? Don't forget to think about your surface area, how streamlined you are, and buoyancy!

GLOSSARY

forces	a push or pull of an object
lift	pulling something upwards
molecules	tiny particles that make up different substances
momentum	how fast an object is moving because of its speed and weight
resist	to push back against something
streamlined	a shape that is less affected by drag and resistance
surface area	the size of the surface of an object
synchronised	a group of people or objects that do the same things at the same time

INDEX